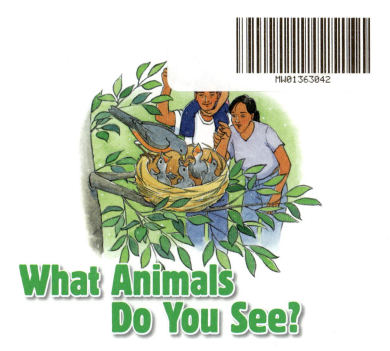

What Animals Do You See?

by Linda B. Ross
illustrated by Phyllis Polema Cahill

Editorial Offices: Glenview, Illinois • Parsippany, New Jersey • New York, New York
Sales Offices: Needham, Massachusetts • Duluth, Georgia • Glenview, Illinois
Coppell, Texas • Ontario, California • Mesa, Arizona

Every effort has been made to secure permission and provide appropriate credit for photographic material. The publisher deeply regrets any omission and pledges to correct errors called to its attention in subsequent editions.

Unless otherwise acknowledged, all photographs are the property of Scott Foresman, a division of Pearson Education.

Photo locators denoted as follows: Top (T), Center (C), Bottom (B), Left (L), Right (R), Background (Bkgd)

Illustrations by Phyllis Polema Cahill

Photograph 8 (B) ©DK Images

ISBN: 0-328-13155-5

Copyright © Pearson Education, Inc.

All Rights Reserved. Printed in the United States of America. This publication is protected by Copyright, and permission should be obtained from the publisher prior to any prohibited reproduction, storage in a retrieval system, or transmission in any form by any means, electronic, mechanical, photocopying, recording, or likewise. For information regarding permission(s), write to: Permissions Department, Scott Foresman, 1900 East Lake Avenue, Glenview, Illinois 60025.

6 7 8 9 10 V010 14 13 12 11 10 09 08 07

Fran, Mom, and Dad went for a walk.

"We can look for animals!" said Fran.

"Look in this log," said Dad.
"What do you see?"

"I can see a frog," said Fran.
"He is eating in this log."

"Look in this tree," said Mom.
"What do you see?"

"I can see small birds," said Fran.
"They are eating in the nest!"

"Look in the woods," said Mom.
"What do you see?"

"I can see a deer," said Fran.
"He is eating here."

"We saw animals eat dinner,"
said Fran.

"Do you want your dinner?"
said Dad.

"I do!" said Fran.

Birds in Nests

Birds live in many different places. No matter where they live, most birds build nests. The mother bird lays her eggs in the nest. She sits on the eggs until they hatch. Then there are baby birds! Soon the baby birds grow up. When they grow up, they will leave the nest.